Pony Pals®

Guide to the Great Outdoors

Scholastic Inc.

New York   Toronto   London   Auckland   Sydney
Mexico City   New Delhi   Hong Kong

ISBN 0-439-06296-9

12 11 10 9 8 7 6 5 4 3   1 2 3 4/0

Printed in the U.S.A.   40
First Scholastic printing, November 1999

CONTENTS

THE GREAT OUTDOORS

In many places, horses and ponies live outdoors all year long. In the Pony Pals® books, Lulu, Pam, and Anna spend as much time as they can outside with their ponies going on trail rides or hikes. They love riding and enjoying nature in the snow as much as they do when the air is warm and the trees are green.

With this book you can have fun observing and learning about nature in every season. You'll find interesting activities, great projects, and fun crafts.

And you don't need a pony
to do any of them!

CHAPTER ONE

FALL

Fall is a wonderful time to be outdoors. In many areas the leaves on the trees are colorful and begin to fall and the air is brisk. Horses and ponies love autumn because it's a time when they are not too hot and there aren't as many insects around to bother them. They get frisky and begin to grow their winter coats.

Fill in the information below.

Name: _____

Grade and age: _____

Year: _____

I love fall because _____

_____

_____

_____.

OUTDOOR JOURNAL I

In the Pony Pals® books, Anna's father travels to exotic places and writes stories about wild animals. He has to have keen observation skills to discover interesting information to write about. Like her dad, Anna keeps her eyes wide open to see things other people might not notice.

You can practice your observation skills, too. Choose a spot near your house. It can even be a place you see from your bedroom window every day. Check your spot every morning, afternoon, or early evening. Or check it more than once a day, if you'd like. Get to know it well and then answer the questions below.

1. Where is your spot?

_____

2. How big is your spot?

_____

3. What trees grow in your spot?

_____

4. What plants grow in your spot?

_____

5. What animals come to your spot?

_____

6. What birds come to your spot?

_____

7. What insects have you seen at your spot?

_____

8. Other things you see at your spot:

(circle any you see)

Birds' nests

Wasps' nests

Pond or stream

Big rocks or boulders

Other:

_____

_____

PLACE A PICTURE HERE

Use this page to draw a picture of your spot, or take a photo of it and glue or tape it here. Label everything you see, from the trees to the rocks to the anthills you find.

My Spot: Fall _____ (fill in the year)

FALL AT MY SPOT: OBSERVATIONS

Use these pages to make notes about what you see at your spot on three different days during the fall. Be sure to write down anything that is interesting or that has changed since the last time you looked at your spot.

Date: _____ Time: _____

Weather: _____

My spot is: (circle)   quiet   busy.

Birds and animals I see: _____

_____

Changes I have noticed since the last time
I checked my spot: _____

_____

_____

The leaves are: (circle)

red   yellow   orange   green   a mixture of colors.

There are more/less leaves on the trees than
(circle)   on the ground.

Date: _____ Time: _____

Weather: _____

My spot is: (circle) quiet   busy.

Birds and animals I see: _____

_____

Changes I have noticed since the last time

I checked my spot: _____

_____

_____

The leaves are: (circle)

red   yellow   orange   green   a mixture of colors.

There are more/less leaves on the trees than
(circle)   on the ground.

Date:_____ Time:_____

Weather: _____

My spot is: (circle)   quiet   busy.

Birds and animals I see: _____

_____

Changes I have noticed since the last time

I checked my spot:_____

_____

_____

The leaves are: (circle)

red   yellow   orange   green   a mixture of colors.

There are more/less leaves on the trees than
(circle)   on the ground.

SAVE THOSE LEAVES!

The colors of autumn leaves can be brilliant and beautiful. Before the fallen leaves turn brown, preserve them and use them as place-setting decorations.

WHAT YOU NEED

Leaves of various colors

Iron (Ask a grown-up to help you.)

Towel

Waxed paper

WHAT YOU DO

1. Take a fall walk and collect the most brilliantly colored leaves you can find.

2. With a grown-up's help, plug in the iron. Turn it to a low setting.

3. Lay the towel on a counter. Cover half the towel with a piece of waxed paper.

4. Place a leaf carefully on the piece of waxed paper. Place another piece of waxed paper on top. Fold the towel carefully over the leaf.

5. Iron the towel over the leaf. Hold the iron down on the towel for 30 seconds. The idea is to melt the wax onto the leaf without burning the towel.

6. Unfold the towel and put the leaf in the waxed paper on a table to cool. Repeat steps 3–5 for each leaf you wish to preserve.

7. Carefully remove the waxed paper from each leaf after it has cooled. Your leaf should feel smooth and a little slippery.

8. Put one leaf at the top of each place setting on the table.

HANG A BIRD FEEDER AT YOUR SPOT

If fall is in the air, then winter can't be far behind! Many wild birds fly south for the winter, but some stay where they are. Food can be hard for them to find during the cold months. You can help the birds get through the winter with this bird feeder. Hang one outside the kitchen or your bedroom window. You can also hang one in your spot, if you like.

WHAT YOU NEED

Five medium-to-big pinecones

Five 12-inch pieces of string

Suet or vegetable shortening (Suet is animal fat. You can get it at the supermarket meat counter or at a butcher shop.)

9 x 13-inch baking dish

Bag of birdseed

Waxed paper

Step #1

Step #2

Step #3 and #4

Steps #3 and #4

WHAT YOU DO

1. Tie one end of each piece of string around the top of each pinecone.

2. Using your fingers, fill the spaces in the pinecones with suet or shortening.

3. Fill the baking dish with birdseed.

4. Keeping the string out of the way, roll each pinecone in the seed until it's coated. Lay the finished pinecone on a piece of waxed paper.

5. Tie your pinecones to the branches of a bush or tree so they hang.

Note: Some birds don't like to eat perched on a bird feeder. Bring some extra birdseed and scatter it on the ground or on a rock for these birds.

WOODPECKER FEEDER

Woodpeckers love suet just on its own. Here's a feeder you can make that will attract these birds.

WHAT YOU NEED

Net bag (Oranges are often packed in net bags. So are onions, and foil-wrapped chocolate coins.)

Suet

Twist tie

12-inch-long piece of string

WHAT YOU DO

1. Open the net bag and put a chunk of suet inside.

2. Gather the bag together so that it is tight around the suet chunk.

3. Close it with the twist tie.

4. Push the string through the netting and tie the ends around the branch of a tree.

Important Note: Once you start feeding the birds, you need to keep feeding them all through the fall and winter until spring. They will come to rely on you for food.

TYPES OF BIRDS THAT FEED AT MY FEEDER

Keep an eye on your bird feeder for a week or two and check off which of the birds listed below you have seen. If you see a bird that doesn't match the descriptions below, write your own description. Then, use a bird book to look up what type it is.

Cardinal

Cardinals: birds with bright red feathers, black faces, and red bills

Blue jays: big blue birds

Chickadees: small gray-and-white birds with black capped heads and white cheeks

Blue Jay

Chickadee

Nuthatches: birds with black heads and white breasts that like to walk up tree trunks

Downy woodpeckers: birds with a red spot on their heads and black-and-white wings

Downy Woodpecker

Other birds I've seen:

Description: _____

I think this type of bird is a _____.

Description: _____

I think this type of bird is a _____.

SPOT THE BIRDS' NESTS WALK

In the autumn, the leaves fall from many trees and branches become bare. This is the perfect time of year to look for birds' nests because the lack of leaves make them easier to see. Invite your Pony Pals to join you as you take a walk to look for birds' nests. Make sure you dress warmly enough!

WHAT TO WEAR

Hiking boots or heavy shoes

Warm socks

Long pants

T-shirt under a flannel shirt under a sweater

Hat

Gloves or mittens

Binoculars around your neck

WHAT TO BRING IN YOUR BACKPACK

Extra pair of socks

Extra T-shirt

Snack

Water

Pencil

Camera

This book!

WHERE TO GO

Take your walk anywhere there are trees. You can go to a favorite trail that winds through the woods or walk up a dirt road. You can even walk along paths in your local city park.

HOW TO FIND NESTS

- Look up! Birds build their nests above the ground to keep them away from egg-eating land animals.

- Look between branches! Birds build their nests in the forks of branches.

- Look carefully! Some birds build nests that are small.

- Look closely! Use your binoculars to see the nests in detail—don't get too close or else you could scare away any birds that might be in the nests.

BIRD'S NEST JOURNAL

As you find nests, answer these questions. Use your binoculars to get a closer look.

1. How high off the ground do you think the nest is?_____

   _____

2. What is the nest made of? Circle the items you can see through your binoculars:

String	Hair
Straw	Twigs
Grass	Plastic strips

   Other:_____

3. Do you think the nest is hidden well when there are leaves on the tree?_____

   _____

4. What kind of bird do you think made this nest?

   _____

5. Look on the ground under the tree. Are there any eggshells there? If so, what do they look like?_____

   _____

6. Draw a picture or tape a photograph of the nest here.

MAKE YOUR OWN BIRD'S NEST

Create your own bird's nest that you can keep in your room or anywhere you want to add a rustic touch.

WHAT YOU NEED

Nine brown or white pipe cleaners   Plastic strips

Long, dry grass   Twigs

Straw or hay   Hair

WHAT YOU DO

1. Make a circle with two pipe cleaners by bending each one into a half circle and twisting the ends together. The circle should be about three inches in diameter, which is the average size of a bird's nest.

2. Twist the end of another pipe cleaner around the edge of the circle, and twist the other end around the opposite side, leaving it curved outward. Repeat this three more times moving around the circle. It should make a little bowl shape.

3. Starting at the bottom, twist the end of another pipe cleaner around the center where all the other pipe cleaners come together. Then weave the pipe cleaner under and over and around the bowl frame. Continue to spiral up and around, weaving in and out of the pipe cleaner frame with the other two pipe cleaners. Twist the end around the rim of the nest.

4. Create your nest. Weave the long pieces of dry grass under and over and through the web of pipe cleaners. Add some hay or straw. Weave in some plastic strips and twigs. Be sure the inside is covered as well as the outside.

Put your nest in a high place in your room. Be sure you are careful with it because there's more to do with it in the spring.

CHAPTER TWO

❄ WINTER ❄

The Pony Pals love to ride through the woods in the winter. Their ponies are shaggy with their thick winter coats, and Pony Pal Trail is covered with snow. Winter is a cool season for walking and watching nature in action. As long as you dress warmly enough, you can see quite a lot of action during the cold part of the year.

WINTER WALK DRESSING TIPS:

- Layering is the way to go. When you wear many layers, they'll keep you warm but then you can always take something off if you get hot from walking. Start with a T-shirt. Follow with a long-sleeved shirt, a wool sweater, and a coat. Wear long johns under your pants. Wool is excellent material for pants because it's warm even when it's damp. Wearing two pairs of socks is a good idea, too. Liners and mittens will keep your hands warm.

- Wear a scarf. If your neck is warm, you will be warm. You can also wrap a scarf around your face if the wind picks up.

- Wear a hat. An incredible amount of heat leaves your body through your head. A hat keeps your body heat in and keeps you warm.

- Wear boots that are roomy enough so the blood can reach your toes easily.

- Carry a snack—something with sugar is good because sugar provides an energy boost. Apples are excellent because they have natural sugars and can also quench your thirst.

- Carry water. In a pinch, you can eat clean snow but it takes a lot of snow to quench your thirst (and sometimes it's hard to tell if the snow is clean).

THE SCIENCE OF LAYERING

Layers of clothes on us act like a pony's fur coat. Air gets trapped between the layers the way air is trapped between the hairs of a pony's coat. Your body heat warms that air and acts as insulation against the cold outside.

❄ EVERGREEN WREATH ❄

In winter, when other trees are bare, evergreens are still green. This is because they have needles that don't fall off instead of leaves. You can use evergreen boughs to make a pretty, festive wreath. If you don'tknow what an evergreen looks like, look it up in an encyclopedia so you'll know what you are searching for.

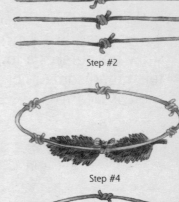

Step #2

WHAT YOU NEED

Six pipe cleaners

Approximately ten pieces (6–8 inches long each) of evergreen branch

Ten 4-inch pieces of green-and-red-plaid ribbon

Small bell on a string

3-inch piece of yarn

Step #4

Step #5

Steps #7 and #8

WHAT YOU DO

1. Take a walk outside in a park or through the woods. Break small branches off evergreen trees. The ends of the branches are thin and flexible and should be easy to break off. Bring the branches home.

2. Twist the ends of two pipe cleaners together. Twist the other two pairs together in the same way.

3. Twist the ends of the three pieces together to join all the pipe cleaners and form a circle.

4. Lay a branch along a part of the circle. Tie it in place with a piece of ribbon.

5. Lay another branch the opposite way. Tie it on, too.

6. Keep on laying branches in opposite directions and tying them to the pipe cleaners until the whole circle is covered with branches.

7. Tie the bell to the bottom of the wreath.

8. Tie the piece of yarn to the top of the wreath.

Hang your wreath on your door or in your window!

❄ TRACKING TRACKS ❄

When there's snow, it becomes easier to find
animal tracks. Go somewhere the snow is relatively
untrampled and look at the ground to find tracks.
Every animal leaves a different kind of footprint.
A mouse's tracks don't look anything like a bird's
tracks or like your own tracks. Compare the tracks
below with tracks you see in the woods, in a park,
or in your spot.

Mouse   Cat

Chipmunk   Dog

Squirrel   Bird

Rabbit   Horse

Deer

Circle the tracks you find and write down any observations you have about them.

_____

_____

_____

_____

Other tracks: If you see tracks that don't look look like ones on the facing page draw what the tracks look like here.

What animal do you think made these tracks?

_____

ANIMAL TRACKS MEDALLION NECKLACES

You can wear the tracks of your favorite animals around your neck by making cool pendant necklaces.

WHAT YOU NEED

Modeling dough
  (see recipe on page 28)

Chopstick

Poster paint

Rolling pin

Small drinking glass

Clear nail polish

Paintbrush

26-inch-long piece of ¼-inch-thick satin ribbon in any color or colors (You can also use yarn.)

WHAT YOU DO

1. Mix the modeling dough according to the directions in the recipe on page 28.

2. Roll out the dough with the rolling pin until it's about ¼-inch thick.

3. Use the glass to cut out as many medallions as you want. (A medallion is like a pendant—it's usually round with words or decorations on it and it hangs from a ribbon or yarn and is worn around your neck.) With the chopstick make a hole near the edge of each medallion. The ribbon will go through this hole.

4. Press or carve tracks into each medallion. Check the tracks on page 29 to find out how to make some different types of animal tracks.

5. Place the medallions on a clean surface and let them dry. This will take a few hours.

6. When the medallions are completely dry, brush them with clear nail polish and let dry. For a glittering snow effect, brush with clear sparkle nail polish. Give them two or three coats. You can also paint the medallions different colors using poster paint.

7. When the polish or paint is dry, run a 26-inch piece of ribbon or yarn through each medallion's hole and tie the ends together in a knot.

Animal tracks medallions make great gifts for your friends!

Leftover Dough Idea: Knead the leftover dough into a big lump and then make a sculpture of one of the animals whose tracks you painted.

❄ RECIPE: MODELING DOUGH ❄

WHAT YOU NEED

1 cup baking soda	Saucepan
$1/2$ cup cornstarch	Wooden spoon
$2/3$ cup of warm water	Cutting board
Measuring cup	Food coloring (optional)

WHAT YOU DO

1. Put the baking soda and cornstarch in the saucepan. Mix with the wooden spoon.

2. Add water and stir everything until it's smooth.

3. Ask a grown-up to help you turn the stove burner on to medium.

4. Put the saucepan on the burner and bring the mixture to a boil. Cook for approximately 15 minutes, stirring constantly, until the compound looks like mashed potatoes. Take the mixture off the heat.

5. Ask a grown-up to help you carefully pour the compound onto the cutting board. Let it cool.

6. When it's cool enough to handle, knead it with your fingers. Now it's ready to be made into Animal Tracks Medallion Necklaces.

Clay color: If you like, you can knead food coloring into the clay at this time to make different colors.

❄ **TRACKS** ❄

You can press and carve some tracks right into the medallion by using these devices:

Horse: Create a horseshoe print by pressing the end of a Popsicle stick into the compound. You can also bend open a paper clip a little bit and use the rounded end of it to make a horseshoe print.

Bird: Use the tip of a butter knife to make Vs, then cut lines through the middle of the Vs to create bird tracks.

All-purpose Paw Prints: Use the end of a chopstick to make circles in the compound. Then use the tip of a toothpick to make toe prints around the top edge of the circles.

Human Footprint: Press a doll's bare foot into the compound.

Winter isn't the only season when you can find tracks. You can find tracks in the mud during spring and fall and in the sand and dirt of summer, too.

WINTER AT MY SPOT: ❄ OBSERVATIONS

What is the cold season like at your spot? Take a walk to your spot three different times during the winter and answer the questions below to record what you observe.

Date:_____Time:_____

Weather: _____

Is there snow everywhere? If not, which spots have no snow? Why do you think these patches are bare? Or, if you live in a warm place that doesn't get snow, describe what changes you do see from the fall.

_____

_____

Are there any animal tracks? If so, what do they look like? What animal do you think made them?

_____

_____

Is all the birdseed that you put out gone? _____

Don't forget to scatter more seed each time out before you leave your spot!

Date:_____ Time:_____

Weather: _____

Is there snow everywhere? If not, which spots have no snow? Why do you think these patches are bare? Or, if you live in a warm place that doesn't get snow, describe what changes you do see from the fall.

_____

_____

Are there any animal tracks? If so, what do they look like? What animal do you think made them?

_____

_____

Is all the birdseed that you put out gone? _____

Don't forget to scatter more seed each time out before you leave your spot!

Date: _____ Time: _____

Weather: _____

Is there snow everywhere? If not, which spots
have no snow? Why do you think these patches
are bare? Or, if you live in a warm place that
doesn't get snow, describe what changes you do
see from the fall.

_____

_____

Are there any animal tracks? If so, what do they
look like? What animal do you think made them?

_____

_____

Is all the birdseed that you put out gone? _____

Don't forget to scatter more seed each time out
before you leave your spot!

❄ TAKE THE CHIPMUNK/ ❄ SQUIRREL TEST

Does a squirrel or chipmunk visit your spot?
Here's how you can find out:

- Leave walnuts or any other kind of nut in their shells on a rock on the ground.

- Check your spot quietly and often. Are any of the nuts gone? If so, there has probably been a chipmunk or squirrel visiting your spot! If you're patient, you may even get to see little critters collecting or eating the nuts—they hold the nuts in their hands and use their incredibly sharp teeth to slice through the shells.

Draw a picture or paste a photograph of your spot in the winter to the right.

Date:_____

I love winter because _____

_____.

❄ PONY ORNAMENT ❄

Make this "pony pal" to hang on your Christmas tree or in your window.

WHAT YOU NEED

3-inch cardboard tube

Thin cardboard

Pencil

Scissors

Crayons or markers

Six 3-inch pieces of yarn

Ten 1-inch pieces of yarn

Two ½-inch pieces of yarn

Paper clip

Glue

7-inch piece of ribbon or yarn

WHAT YOU DO

1. Place one end of the cardboard tube on the piece of cardboard.

2. Trace around the tube with the pencil. Move it over a few inches and trace around it again, so you have two circles side by side.

3. Draw your pony's head and front legs around one circle and its rear end and legs around the other as shown.

4. Cut out the parts and color them. Put the eyes and nostrils on the pony's face. Does your pony have markings on its legs? If so, add those, too.

5. Poke a hole in the rear end using the scissors. Thread the six 3-inch pieces of yarn through the hole and tie knots so the yarn won't slip out. This is your tail.

6. Glue the 1-inch pieces of yarn on the pony's neck for the mane and the $1/2$-inch pieces on the pony's forehead for the forelock.

7. Color the cardboard tube the same color as the rest of your pony. Poke two holes about $1/2$-inch apart in your pony's back halfway along the tube.

8. Unbend the paper clip. Make a small hook at both ends. Push one end through one hole and the other end through the other hole.

9. Tie the ribbon or yarn to the center of the paper clip. This is for hanging your pony pal.

10. Glue the front and rear ends of your pony onto the ends of the cardboard tube. Stand the pony on his head or tail to dry.

CHAPTER THREE

✿ SPRING ✿

Spring is a wonderful time to be outdoors watching nature awaken after a quiet, dormant winter. The snow is melting, a light green glow can be seen on the trees as the fresh, young buds open, and horses and ponies start to shed their thick winter coats. The Pony Pals use shedding blades—special grooming tools—to help their ponies lose their shaggy layer. Ponies sometimes roll in the spring mud because shedding is itchy and this helps them scratch. The hair that comes off is often used by birds in their nests.

✿ MAPLE SYRUP TIME ✿

In spring, the sap in trees starts running. Sap is like blood for trees—it runs through them, bringing food that helps them grow. The sap from sugar maple trees is sweet and is used to make maple syrup. People put taps in the trees, the sap drips out into buckets, and then the sap is boiled down until it becomes syrup.

Take a walk outside and look for maple trees. Remember, spring can be wet so bring along a dry pair of socks in your pack!

IDENTIFY A SUGAR MAPLE TREE

- **Bark:** Sugar maple trees can grow up to 120 feet high and their bark is light gray-brown with fine ridges.

- **Buds:** Even in earliest spring, the buds on a sugar maple are big and thick.

- **Leaves:** Sugar maple leaves have five points. If the leaves are already out, that means the time for making maple syrup is over.

❄ SUGAR ON SNOW ❄

In Vermont after the syrup is made there is traditionally a "sugar on snow" party. Before the last of the snow melts, people dribble thickened maple syrup that has been cooked an extra-long time onto the snow—the syrup then hardens on the snow and can be removed and eaten like candy. Even if you don't tap your own maple trees, you can have your own version of a "sugar on snow" party to celebrate the beginning of spring.

WHAT YOU NEED

Snow   Bowl   Maple syrup   Teaspoon

WHAT YOU DO

1. Make a snowball using fresh clean snow.
2. Put the snowball in the bowl.
3. Pour some maple syrup on top of the snowball. Eat it and enjoy! (You can also use vanilla ice cream.)

❊ WELCOME BACK, BIRDS ❊

It really is true that you can always tell it's spring by the return of the robins. Here's how to make your own pretty paper robin to put in the nest that you made earlier in the book (pp. 18–19).

ORIGAMI ROBIN

WHAT YOU NEED

9 x 9-inch square of white blank paper
  (Make sure the paper isn't too heavy.)

Scissors   Crayons

WHAT YOU DO

1. Fold the square in half to form a triangle. (Fig. 1)

2. Fold it in half again to form a smaller triangle. (Fig. 2)

3. Lift one side of the triangle and fold it down to form a square. (Fig. 3)

4. Repeat with the other side. (Fig.4)

5. Hold the square so the open point is facing you. Lift the top of the square so the paper forms an open "mouth" shape. Fold the bottom edges from both sides of the "mouth" into the middle. Then lift the

top of the
square up
and back
continuing to
fold in the two
sides as you go.
(Fig. 5) You will have
a diamond shape.

6. Flip and
repeat. You
will end up
with a long
diamond
shape. (Fig. 6)

7. Fold the top
points of the
diamond
down to
form a kite
shape. (Fig. 7)

8. Fold the kite in
half lengthwise.
(Fig. 8)

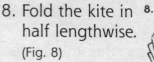

9. Cut the top fold
<u>only</u> halfway
up, then fold the cut
pieces up to form
wings. Then
fold the
other end in
and down to
form the
head and
beak. (Fig. 9)

10. Color the breast red.
Color the body
brown. Add eyes.

Place the origami bird in
the nest.

Baby Birds: You can make
smaller robins by starting
with smaller squares.
Experiment until you find
the right size.

❊ SPRING WALK ❊

Spring is the time to watch the world awaken. As the sun gets warmer and the days get longer, buds open, animals emerge from their dens, and people come out of their houses. The warm sun and rain means there's lots of mud! And though the weather is milder, it can still be pretty chilly. So be prepared when you venture outside. Here's a list of things to take on a spring walk.

WHAT TO WEAR

Waterproof shoes

Long pants

Cap or hat

Heavy cotton socks

Short-sleeved shirt under a long-sleeved shirt

WHAT TO BRING IN YOUR BACKPACK

Water

Windbreaker

Pair of cotton gloves

Your camera

Snack

Extra pair of socks

Pen or pencil

This book!

❀ SPRING AT MY SPOT: ❀ OBSERVATIONS

Use these pages to make notes about what you see at your spot three different times you visit it. Be sure to write down anything that's different or that changes over the course of time.

Date:_____ Time:_____

Weather:_____

My spot is: quiet   busy   muddy   wet. (circle one)

Birds and animals I see:_____

_____

Changes I have noticed since the last time I checked

my spot:_____

_____

There are   buds   leaves   on the trees. (circle)

I see   crocuses   daffodils   skunk cabbage. (circle)

Other plants and flowers I see: _____

Do you see any birds' nests?_____

Where are they? _____

Do birds live in them? _____

Date:_____ Time:_____

Weather: _____

My spot is: quiet busy muddy wet. (circle one)

Birds and animals I see:_____

_____

Changes I have noticed since the last time I

checked my spot:_____

_____

There are buds leaves on the trees. (circle)

I see crocuses daffodils skunk cabbage. (circle)

Other plants and flowers I see: _____

Do you see any birds' nests?_____

Where are they? _____

Do birds live in them? _____

Date:_____ Time:_____

Weather: _____

My spot is: quiet busy muddy wet. (circle one)

Birds and animals I see:_____

_____

Changes I have noticed since the last time I

checked my spot:_____

_____

There are buds leaves on the trees. (circle)

I see crocuses daffodils skunk cabbage. (circle)

Other plants and flowers I see: _____

Do you see any birds' nests?_____

Where are they? _____

Do birds live in them? _____

Draw a picture or tape a photograph
of your spot here.

Date:_____.

I love spring because_____.

Bird Feeder Note: Now is the time to take
down your bird feeder. In spring, birds can find
the worms and insects they like to eat much
more easily.

❀ POND PATROL ❀

Spring is the season of water. Puddles and ponds pop up everywhere due to melting snow and spring showers. This is when life in ponds begins. Take a hike in the woods, or along a dirt road, or through a city park to see what watery signs of spring you can observe.

Find a body of water—a pond, stream, or lake—and then answer these questions:

1. Look at the water. Do you see any signs of movement? Look for circles in the water or bubbles. What do you see? _____

   _____

2. Stop walking, close your eyes, and listen for a few minutes—what do you hear?

   (Circle any things you hear.)

   Frogs

   Birds

   Insects

   Fish splashing in and out of water

   Other: _____

JEEPERS PEEPERS

If you're in the country in the spring, you might be able to hear the peepers sing at night. Peepers are little frogs that live in ponds. They're named after the sound they make. The high peeping sound of this little amphibian means spring is really here.

3. Now open your eyes, walk, and listen some more. As you walk, what other sounds do you hear? _____

_____

4. Can you see what's making the sounds? What do you see?_____

_____

5. Squat down by the water's edge. What do you see either in the water or at the edge, on land?

_____

_____

EGG ALERT

In addition to tadpoles and little frogs, you might also find some frog's eggs if you are looking in a pond. Here's what to look for:

- Frog's eggs are clear, round, and bubble-like.

- They have a dark spot at the center.

- They float in clusters, like grapes, near the edge of a pond.

❀ NEST-WATCHING SPRING STYLE ❀

Spring is the season of birth. The birds who return from their winter homes get together back at their nests to produce eggs. Take a walk around and look at the nests you found in the fall. Have any birds moved back in? One way to find out is by watching the birds. You can locate their nests by observing where they fly to and from, and where they land in the trees.

What kind of birds do you see?

_____

_____

_____

Where do they fly to?

_____

_____

_____

Where is the nest?

_____

_____

_____

Here's a way you can make some eggs to put in your nest along with the origami robin to complete the whole nest scene.

WHAT YOU NEED

Scissors

Sheet of newspaper

Glue

Two small paintbrushes

Blue, light green, and brown paint

WHAT YOU DO

1. Cut out a 3 x 3-inch square of newspaper for each egg you want to make.

2. Crumple it into a tight ball.

3. Cut ½-inch strips of newspaper about 6 inches long.

Step #1

4. Spread glue on these strips. Wrap them around the crumpled paper. Shape the wrapped ball into an oval.

Step #2

5. Let dry for a few hours.

6. Paint the eggs. Robins' eggs are light blue with small brown speckles. Other birds have light green and brown eggs.

Step #3

Put the eggs in your nest and put the origami robin on top.

Step #4

CHAPTER FOUR

ᐳ SUMMER ᐳ

The Pony Pals take full advantage of summer—
they ride their ponies whenever they can, they
have picnics by bubbling brooks, and they sleep
in the hayloft with the summer stars above.

Summer is the easiest season to go outside and
observe nature. You don't need to bundle up.
The world is active with living creatures. Ponies
and horses graze freely in green pastures and
their sleek, dappled coats shine. But like every
other season, summer has two sides to it.

There are bugs that bite and flies that buzz in
ponies' eyes, and sometimes it's just too hot
to do much of anything.
How do you feel about
summer? Fill in the
chart on the next page
withall of the reasons
you love (or don't
love!) summer.

WHAT I LOVE ABOUT SUMMER

_____

_____

_____

_____

_____

_____

_____

_____

_____

_____

_____

WHAT I HATE ABOUT SUMMER

_____

_____

_____

_____

_____

_____

_____

_____

_____

_____

_____

SUMMER AT MY SPOT

You can spend a lot of time hanging out at your spot when the weather's nice. You can even bring your friends and have a picnic there!

WHAT TO WEAR

Sneakers or hiking boots

White cotton socks

Shorts with pockets

T-shirt

Bandanna tied around your neck (If you get too hot, you can soak the bandanna in cool water and wipe your face, then tie it wet around your neck again.)

Cap with a visor

WHAT TO PACK

Water

Lunch

Sunglasses

Sunscreen

Vinyl sweatpants

Pair of dry socks

Pencil

Camera

This book!

❦ OBSERVATIONS ❦

Use the following pages to record your observations of your spot at three different times during the summer.

Date: _____ Time: _____

Weather: _____

Take a quick look around. What's the first thing you notice? _____

_____

Now look around more slowly. What else do you see? _____

_____

Do you see any birds' nests? _____

If so, what kind of birds do you think live in the nests? _____

_____

Are there flowers around? _____

What do they look like? _____

Draw them.

Date:_____ Time:_____

Weather: _____

Take a quick look around. What's the first thing
you notice?_____

_____

Now look around more slowly. What else do
you see?_____

_____

Do you see any birds' nests? _____

If so, what kind of birds do you think live in the
nests? _____

_____

Are there flowers around? _____

What do they look like?_____

Draw them.

Date:_____ Time:_____

Weather: _____

Take a quick look around. What's the first thing
you notice?_____

_____

Now look around more slowly. What else do
you see?_____

_____

Do you see any birds' nests? _____

If so, what kind of birds do you think live in the
nests? _____

_____

Are there flowers around? _____

What do they look like?_____

Draw them.

LATE SUMMER WALK

As you walk, look up, look down, stop, and look around. Write down your observations.

Insects (circle any you see):

Wasp

Ant

Butterflies

Flies

Wasps

Dragonflies

Ants

Bees

Caterpillars

Other: _____

Dragonfly

Caterpillar

Draw any insects that you see. How many legs do they have? Wings? Antennae?

Have lunch. Then sit quietly and just wait and observe. Try not to talk or move too much. Let your spot move around you. As the animals get used to your presence, they will become bolder. Pick a spot within your spot. Observe it closely. Use your eyes as a microscope. See how much detail you can pick out.

Are there any insects on the blades of grass?

Any beetles walking beneath the blades of grass?

Are there seed shells on the ground?

What else do you notice?

_____

_____

_____

_____

Bee

ANIMAL ALERT

Close your eyes and listen.

Do you hear rustling?_____

Chittering? _____

Other noises: _____

Open your eyes. Look around.

What evidence of animals do you see? (circle)

trampled grass?   (This could mean deer.)

nibbled buds?   (This could mean deer, too.)

nibbled grass?   (This could mean rabbits.)

What else do you see that makes you think animals have been to your spot? Any tracks? What animals do you think were there?_____

_____

Do you see any animals now? _____

If so, which ones? _____

Draw a picture of your spot or tape
a photograph of it here.

Date:_____

I love summer because _____.

❧ GRASS WHISTLE ❧

Whenever the Pony Pals go out on a trail ride or a hike, they always carry their whistles with them, which they can blow to attract attention in case they get into trouble and need help.

You should carry a whistle with you whenever you are on your own or with friends. But in case you ever get caught without a whistle and need to get someone's attention, or if you and your friends want an easy way to call each other when you're out exploring, here is a whistle you can make out of a blade of grass. Arrange a special whistle call with your friends, or different calls that mean different things.

WHAT YOU NEED

Thick blade of grass about 5 inches long

WHAT YOU DO

1. Press the sides of your thumbs together with your thumbnails facing your face. The tops and bottoms will touch and you should see a small space between them in the middle.

2. Separate your thumbs. Lay the grass flat along the inside of one of your thumbs. Be sure the grass extends beyond the tips of your thumbs and below the bottom of them.

3. Press your thumbs together as you did above. You should see the edge of the grass in that space between your thumbs.

4. Put that space up to your lips. Blow air through your lips and through the space so it hits the blade of grass. Hopefully, you'll hear a whistle.

If you don't hear a whistle, try these suggestions:

1. Shift the position of your thumbs against your lips.

2. Extend your thumbs a bit to pull the grass tighter between them.

3. Blow harder.

HOW IT WORKS

When the air you blow hits the blade of grass, the blade vibrates, making a sound. You can change the sound by changing how tightly you pull the blade of grass between your fingers.

- *If the tension is less, is the whistle lower or higher?*

- *If the tension is greater, is the whistle lower or higher?*

FLOWER FEST

In summer, flowers bloom everywhere. Daisies. Pansies. Indian paintbrush. Cornflowers. Many grow right along the side of the road as well as in gardens. Here's a way to preserve these beautiful flowers all through the year.

WHAT YOU NEED

Fresh flowers

Three quarts of sterile, dry, fine sand (the kind that's used for a sandbox)

9 $\frac{1}{2}$ x 13$\frac{1}{2}$ x 2-inch baking pan

Flour sifter or wire sieve

Paper towels

Soft brush

* * *

A grown-up to help you

Daisy

Indian Paintbrush

WHAT YOU DO

1. Pick some flowers you love.

2. Put a 1-inch layer of sand in the baking pan. Smooth it with your hand.

3. Place flowers on the sand. Make sure there is sand right under the petals so the petals keep their shape.

4. Using the sifter or sieve, gently sift a 1-inch layer of sand over the flowers.

5. Put the baking pan in the oven. Ask a grown-up to help you turn the oven to 200 degrees F. Bake the flowers and sand for about 1 hour and 15 minutes. Do the Flower Check (read how in the box below) after 1 hour and then again every 15 minutes until the flowers are done.

6. When the flowers look done, remove the pan from the oven and pour off the top layer of sand.

7. Carefully remove the flowers and lay them on a paper towel to cool for an hour or more.

8. Use a soft brush to clean the sand off the cooled flowers.

You can use your dried flowers to decorate stationery, place mats, notebook covers, or to make pretty pictures. Glue them to fabric or cardboard and then frame them.

FLOWER CHECK

Have your grown-up brush a little sand off one corner of the baking pan. If the flowers are damp and droopy, they need to bake longer.

If the flowers are dull and dark, they've been overbaked.

When they are done, your flowers will be dried out but they should look about the same as they did when they were fresh.

FLOWER STORAGE

You can save your flowers for winter crafts and gifts by placing them facedown in a cardboard box.

FLOWER CARDS

You can use your dried flowers to create pretty homemade greeting cards.

WHAT YOU NEED

Construction paper

Flowers

Scissors

Clear contact paper

WHAT YOU DO

1. Fold the construction paper in half the short way to make a card.

2. Arrange the flowers you want to use on the front of the card.

3. Cut the contact paper so it is $1/2$-inch bigger all around than the front of the card.

4. Remove the backing and carefully place the contact paper over the flowers.

5. Cut the excess contact paper from around the card edges.

Now the card is ready for you to write a message inside it.

MONARCHS, MILKWEED, AND MIGRATION

Late summer days are filled with butterflies. They bask in the heat and feed on the nectar from bright flowers. Monarchs are a type of butterfly. They have striking orange-and-black wings. Monarchs make an amazing trip every summer—they fly from Mexico to the United States. Some fly as far north as Alaska.

Monarchs lay eggs after their trip is complete. The eggs hatch into bright yellow-and-black caterpillars, which spend the summer eating leaves and getting fat.

Then the monarch caterpillars find a nice milkweed plant to settle down on.

Milkweeds grow tall. They have a light purple, waxy flower that smells a little bit like lilac. When the flowers are gone, a big pod is left. Late in the summer, the pod opens and tufts of soft milkweed fiber drift through the air.

Monarch caterpillars shed their skin and spin their cocoons on milkweed plants.

ALASKA

UNITED STATES OF AMERICA

MEXICO

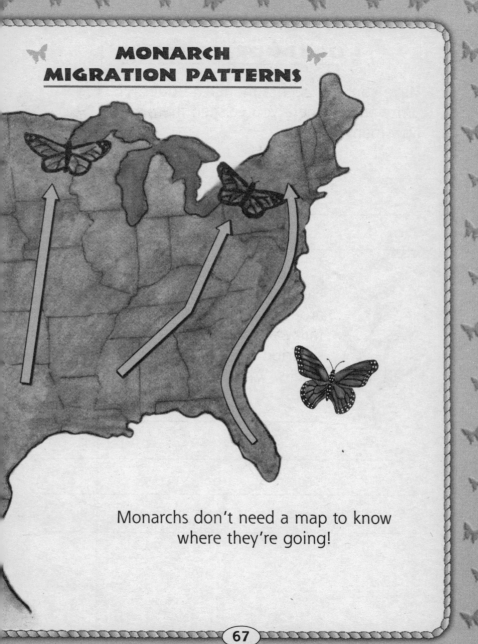

MONARCH MIGRATION PATTERNS

Monarchs don't need a map to know where they're going!

OUTDOOR JOURNAL

Have you ever seen a monarch butterfly? Write about where you've seen them and how many you saw.

_____

_____

_____

Next time you are outside, look around and see if you can find milkweed. If you do see some, describe what it looks like and how it smells. Where did you find the plant?

_____

_____

_____

_____

Look carefully under the milkweed leaves.
Do you see any cocoons?

If so, describe one._____

_____

_____

_____

Check the cocoon often. If possible, try to be there
when it opens and the butterfly comes out.

How did the new monarch look?_____

_____

_____

Were its wings wet or dry? _____

New monarchs sit in the sun for a while to dry out
their wings. Then they flap their wings slowly and
fly away.

BUTTERFLY WALK

Late summer is when adult monarchs die. They can often be found lying beside the road in perfect shape. If you want to collect some butterflies, this is the time to do it.

WHAT YOU NEED

Waxed paper

Cardboard box

WHAT YOU DO

1. Take a walk along the road.

2. Look down.

3. When you find a dead monarch, pick it up carefully by its wing tips.

4. Place it on a piece of waxed paper and fold the paper carefully over it.

5. Place the butterfly in the box.

6. You can put one butterfly on top of another while transporting and storing.

BUTTERFLY DIORAMA

You can give this scene as a nice end-of-summer gift.

WHAT YOU NEED

Scissors

Clean, dry glass jar
with label removed
(Jar should be at
least 16 ounces.)

Paper

Colored pencils

Dirt

Grass

Stones

Twig with a leaf
or two on it

Monarch butterfly

Light wire (You can
use the wire inside
a twist tie.)

Pen

Sticker label about
$\frac{1}{2}$ inch high and
2 inches long

WHAT YOU DO

1. Cut the paper so it is the height of the jar. Cut it again so it fits inside the jar and curves around the back half of the jar only.

2. Draw a background on the piece of paper using colored pencils. Include sky, clouds, trees, and other animals.
   Put the paper in the jar.

3. Put the dirt and grass at the bottom of the jar.

4. Arrange the stones on top of the dirt and grass.

5. Carefully attach the monarch to the branch with the wire.

6. Carefully insert the branch into the jar. Arrange it so it looks realistic.

7. Cover the jar.

8. Give the scene a title, for example, "Monarchs at My Spot."

9. Write the title on the label. Stick the label at the bottom of the jar or on the lid.

Display your butterfly diorama in your room or else give it as a gift!

MONARCHS AT MY SPOT

KEEP EXPLORING!

You've come to the end of your outdoor activity book, but don't let it be the end of your outdoor activities. Many of these activities can be done again and again, season after season. And what's more, once you start exploring and looking for things to do in nature, you'll find all kinds of interesting things! There's something to look at, something to make note of, something to draw or preserve under every rock, in every tree, beside every pond. So keep your eyes open and your notebook ready—and have fun!

EXTRA NOTES AND DRAWINGS

EXTRA NOTES AND DRAWINGS